Richard Nixon

A Richard Nixon

Biography

Anna Revell

Table of Contents

Richard Nixon – Nixongate

Attach the suffix "-gate" to a word and it turns news into a scandal, and scandal into *sensation*.

It creates an accessible buzz-word to encompass what may otherwise be a complex story. Suddenly the talking heads of television, PR spin doctors, op-ed writers, bloggers, social media pundits, your officemates, the average person on the street and perhaps even your grandmother – all rally around a single term to ponder and discuss. When a scandal becomes a "Scandal-gate," it becomes a cultural event that crosses boundaries and absorbs what is usually an attention-deficient public into collective mania and fixation. For a short span of time, we are all speaking the same language.

In 2015, "Deflategate" embroiled the NFL, the New England Patriots and American football legend Tom Brady in a scandal involving the use of underinflated footballs. In Technology, "Gamergate" made the rounds in 2014 about sexism in video game culture. The royal family of the United Kingdom would be shaken by two; the "Squidgygate" tapes of Diana, Princess of Wales speaking with a male friend who called her "Squidgy," and the "Camillagate" tapes of Prince Charles in an intimate conversation with his then-girlfriend, Camilla Parker Bowles. Hollywood wouldn't be immune, with "Celebgate" making the rounds to encompass hacking and leakage of revealing celebrity pictures in 2014.

United States politics, as home of the original "-gate," would unsurprisingly have several scandals labeled as such, among them 2016's "Pussygate" (where then-presidential candidate Donald Trump and TV presenter Billy Bush were caught on tape in 2005, having an vulgar conversation about women, famously including the words, "...*grab them by the pussy.*") and the 1990's iconic "Monicagate," named after the intern who had an inappropriate relationship with then-President Bill Clinton.

Donald Trump would still win the presidency, and Bill Clinton would still get to keep it after their respective "-gate"-worthy misadventures. But the man who is intimately linked to the origin of this phenomenon, who is inextricably part of this enduring addition to our global lexicon, would lose it all – the presidency and control of his legacy. That man is Richard Nixon.

The world at large have a quick understanding of the magnitude of an event the moment a "-gate" is added to its end. Fewer would be able to explain its origins in the Watergate scandal of the early 1970s. Fewer still would be able to say much else about the United States President it ultimately brought to ruin, Richard Nixon.

This is the story of an ambitious, scrappy kid overcoming humble origins to somehow become The Most Powerful Man in the World at a time when the United States was at the top of the global totem pole. This is the story of a man who was an advocate for peace and first to make major breakthroughs to pierce the Iron Curtain of a divided world. The story of a man who steered America at a time of heady, history-making change… who has since been largely reduced to a cartoon caricature, a Halloween mask, and trivia answer with a title no one wants to ever hold: The Only U.S. President Ever to Resign from Office.

This is the story of former U.S. President Richard Nixon beyond Watergate. This is Richard Nixon, revealed, a sensation even without the event that pushed him out of office and that he would always be known for. This is Nixongate – the scandal! the revelation! that there is more to a man than the biggest of his mistakes.

Early Years

Richard Milhous Nixon was born on the 9th of January, 1913 in Yorba Linda, California. He was the second of Frank and Hannah's five male children. They were not wealthy; Frank Nixon had a small lemon ranch and ran a service station with which to support his family. President Nixon would later describe the family as *"poor, but the glory of it was we didn't know it."*

One of the most influential people in President Nixon's life was his mother, Hannah, a Quaker - or a member of the Religious Society of Friends, as the movement is formally known. Dick's father, Frank, initially came from a Methodist background but became part of a Quaker congregation after marrying Hannah. He wouldn't be the only one Hannah would steer toward the precepts of the movement; the future President and his siblings reportedly received religious instruction through a Friends Sunday School while they were children, and "Dick" himself would go on to attend a Quaker-affiliated college when he got older.

The religion of a United States President has always been a concern of the public. Whether or not religious affiliation should be one of the factors considered by voters in electing a man to the highest office of the land is immaterial; many simply do. It is perceived as a barometer for who the president may surround himself with, and the kinds of policies and causes he may champion based on what his conscience considers to be the right thing to do.

Quakers are part of a religious group with Christian roots, though not necessarily identified as Christian. Essentially, they hold that God is love, that His light can be found within every person, that religious experience can be direct rather than ritual or hierarchy-based, and consequently, that religion is inextricable from everyday life and experience. They identify with values of peace and tolerance, human rights causes, social justice and a sense of community.

It is interesting then, how a man who would eventually be shamefully compelled to leave office for political misbehavior would theoretically have such a view of the world. This is just one of the many contradictions in

Nixon's political and spiritual life, but all of that would come into play much later.

In the meantime, Hannah Milhous Nixon is widely regarded as one of the most powerful influences in his life. In one letter addressed to his mother, written when the future President of the United States ("POTUS") was just ten years old, he had actually signed it as *"Your good dog, Richard."*

Hannah, who had been described in the press as a "Quaker saint" but also "emotionally austere," passed away in 1967. In 1971, then-President Richard Nixon dedicated a plaque in her honor, erected in her birthplace of rural Indiana. He was already Commander-in-Chief at the time, creating a stir when he made the rare move of visiting the small town of Vernon. He recalled his late mother's convictions in a speech, where he encouraged people to keep their religious faith, and described how powerful it could be in getting one through tough times. He also spoke of the pursuit of peace, and how he felt it was possible in the coming generation and a task for American leadership to achieve. It was a timely message for a nation caught in the quagmire of the Vietnam War.

Echoes of Hannah, and of the strength that sustained her through difficult times, would be found along the biography and political portfolio of her son, Richard. The family did not have an easy life. Their ranch failed in 1922, prompting them to move to Whittier from Yorba Linda, and put up a service station where the whole family was expected to contribute to make ends meet. Two of

Richard's siblings would die early under tragic circumstances, too. In 1925, one of his younger brothers, Arthur Burdg Nixon, passed away from tubercular encephalitis at only seven years old. Less than a decade later, his beloved older brother, Harold Samuel Nixon, would die from tuberculosis in 1933 at the age of 23.

The future President somehow managed to focus his energies, convictions and ambitions into his schooling and the beginnings of a political career geared for the stratosphere. The start was humbling – he transferred to Whittier High School from Fullerton High School, and lost to another student in his bid for student body president. But he eventually graduated third in his class, with accomplishments good enough to win him a place of scholarship at prestigious Harvard

University – except his family did not have the funds for travel or to sustain his potential living expenses. Foregoing the glittering promise of Harvard, he would settle with the local Quaker institution, Whittier College, in 1930. There, his sense of ambition would not be tarnished.

In Whittier College, Nixon was still an outstanding achiever – debater, athlete and drama production standout, all while helping out in his family's store. He was student body president before his 1934 graduation, and had founded and been president of the fraternity, Orthogonians. The promising young man would again merit a scholarship offer, this time from Duke University Law School in Durham, North Carolina. In Duke, he was relentless in his climb to the top too; he headed the

Student Bar Association, was a member of the law review, and as he was wont to, graduated in the upper levels of his class in 1937.

His triumph at Duke would have him returning to Whittier as an attorney with the oldest law firm in the city, Wingert and Bewley. The ambitious young man was reportedly not quite satisfied about this turn in his career – he was living over his family's garage, back in a life he had worked hard to leave behind. But his homecoming put him in the path of stunning schoolteacher Thelma Catherine Ryan- "Pat," as she was better known then and would be known the world over after her husband became the President of the United States.

It was 1938, and there was a tryout for acting slots in the play "Dark Tower," under production from the local community theater, Whittier Community Players. But the part Richard Nixon apparently really wanted to play, was that of Pat Ryan's husband.

An Irish Gypsy Enters the Scene

Pat Nixon, future First Lady of the United States ("FLOTUS"), was born Thelma Catherine Ryan on the 16th of March, 1912 in the mining town of Ely, Nevada. Her moniker "Pat," as she would eventually be known the world over, was courtesy of her father, William. William had Irish roots, and noted that his daughter's birthday fell on the eve of St. Patrick's Day.

Like the man who would one day be her husband, Pat had humble origins and an early life characterized by struggle. The family was not well off, and eventually moved away from Ely to settle in Artesia, California, where the family started a truck farm. They grew produce and sold them in nearby cities from the back of a truck. The whole family was involved in the enterprise, including planting and harvesting.

Tragedy struck when Pat was barely in her teens. Her mother was debilitated by, and would eventually succumb to, cancer. It wasn't only an emotional drain for a young girl; Pat was also household manager and caregiver to her ailing mom, on top of cooking, cleaning, laundry chores and her responsibilities to the farm.

Her father would die of disease just five years later, perishing from silicosis, a disease linked to mining. While he struggled with his illness, Pat ran the household, continued with farming chores, and took on jobs to cover his medical expenses. The hardy young girl juggled her home and family obligations with early janitorial work at a bank, as well as attending high school and working afterwards as a bookkeeper. She was barely 18 years old and already heavily burdened by care of her family.

How she found time and energy is a mystery. Throughout these hardships, the driven young woman had a lot of pursuits in school, too. When she attended Excelsior High School from 1925-1929, she was in the drama club, the debating team and student government. She would go on to attend courses in Woodbury College in 1929, and Fullerton Junior College from 1931-1932.

A fateful cross-country drive in the year 1932 would bring her to the east, where she found employment at Seton Hospital for the Tubercular. Here, she was able to live and do miscellaneous work, and ultimately save money for further education. Her hard work would eventually find her taking a summer radiology course in Columbia University in New York in 1933, and as a student at the University of Southern California from 1934-1937. Her USC schedule was a grueling one. She was on scholarship, but also worked as assistant to a professor as well as the university's vice president, on a top of a miscellany of jobs including waitress, librarian, product tester, and movie extra. She managed to finish with a B.S.

Merchandising degree, along with a certificate to teach up to the high school level. She graduated cum laude in 1937, and with an equivalent of a master's degree, to boot. She would be the first FLOTUS to have a graduate degree.

Pat was employed as a teacher at Whittier Union High School, where she worked from 1937 until 1941. When she wasn't teaching business courses or shorthand and typing, she indulged her interest in the performing arts by auditioning in a local play – where she would meet another hardy and promising individual, recent law school grad and practicing lawyer, Richard Nixon.

By many accounts, the future President of the United States was smitten right away. As for Pat – love at first sight and immediate attraction was not quite the case. Pat was a beautiful 25-year-old, glamorous, and finally enjoying a sense of independence after years of hardship and supporting her family. Nixon pursued her, but she was too "busy" to date him, and had reportedly once laughed at young Dick's bold claim that he would someday marry her. If later accounts are to be believed, the POTUS-to-be had even driven her to other dates! He drove her about whenever she needed it, and had reportedly bloodied himself ice-skating because she enjoyed the activity with friends. She even avoided contacting him for months at one point, but the driven Dick would not be derailed. He tracked her down and angled for a second chance.

This may seem hard to believe, as the President would eventually be known for not quite being open with his affections for his wife. As a matter of fact, "snub" would be a word used in describing his public interactions with her, with "loveless" not too far behind when outsiders looked at their seemingly frosty relationship. But in keeping with the image of that smitten young lawyer who was sure he'd found The One, Richard Nixon was actually a romantic behind closed doors, at least in their courtship and early in marriage. By 1939, Pat had fallen for the persistent young man too, and they married on the 21st of June, 1940, at the Mission Inn in Riverside, California.

Some of Richard Nixon's love letters to his wife would be displayed publicly later, with one shown in 2012 describing the object of his affection as "*an Irish gypsy*," and including heady language like "*his heart was filled with that great poetic music…"* They exchanged frequent and passionate letters. Those written when they were already married, but during time apart along the course of Dick's training and distant assignments, were especially expressive of their connection and longing. *"I may not say much when I am with you,"* he conceded in one letter, *"but all of me loves you all the time."* In another: *"I think of you when I see beautiful things."*

A Man in Uniform

Happily married, small town lawyer apparently wasn't quite the vision of Richard Nixon had of himself, however. By 1942, the couple would be in Washington, D.C., with Richard working in President Roosevelt's Office of Price Administration. He quickly realized that this was not the future he had in mind, either. His time there would expose him to the shortcomings of government bureaucracy, which would later influence the policies of his latter political career. Later in the year, the ambitious Nixon would be angling for another change.

He had exemption from military service by virtue of his work with the OPA, as well as through his religious affiliation as a Quaker. He would waive this exemption, however, and take a commission with the United States Navy. How this reconciles with a Quaker's belief in peace is unknown; he had never claimed to being a pacifist. But at any rate, this wouldn't be the last of the ways his life would contradict the principles of his known religious affiliation.

His original assignment was at a naval station air base in Ottumwa, Iowa, and Pat found work in a bank there. But Richard would soon request a transfer from the rural cornfields to the South Pacific theater, after seeing a listing on available immediate sea duties for officers. He headed for the war zone in 1943. His request for a transfer would move him to New Caledonia, an archipelago thousands of miles from Australia. Here, he served with the Combat Air Transport Command. Latter assignments would bring him to other distant locales like Bougainville and Green Island. His work entailed preparing flight plans for cargo and transport planes, ordering supplies, and helping with the evacuation of the wounded and the dead.

His wife, Pat, on the other end of the world, settled in San Francisco where there were great job opportunities. She was employed with the Office of Price Administration as an economist. Dick was extremely proud of his wife's posting there, once writing that "*I like to tell the gang how smart you are…*"

Richard Nixon, as aviation ground officer, never saw combat during World War II, and reportedly found his work away from the action to be dull. He wanted to be assigned to a posting where he could contribute more, but he still managed to distinguish himself where he was. By the time he returned to the United States, he had two service stars and a number of commendations. He resigned his commission in 1946, having risen to the rank of lieutenant commander. He left the navy with a few unsavory habits, among them drinking, swearing and smoking. One skill he picked up that would be useful in his future as a politician, however, was poker. He was revealed to be a great bluffer, and was rumored to have won enough funds to help jumpstart his first run for congress.

When the war ended, Richard and Pat reunited and the hardy pair set off for a new endeavor. This project was a perfect place to channel their wellspring of energy and drive. It was an undertaking that may finally be worthy of their hard work and lofty ambitions: American Politics.

Political Life

By 1946, World War II was over and Richard Nixon was back in the arms of his wife – and the life of a civilian. All his life he had hungered for something more, and for a time he found it in the call of military service, with a posting that he still eventually found lacking. What could the new, post-war America possibly hold for the future of an ambitious, intelligent, irrepressible man with grit and daring?

Running for office may seem like the ultimate, appropriate outlet for someone of his single-minded determination and hungry sense of purpose. But the rest of his temperament, if observations by scholars, biographers and his contemporaries are to be believed, was not quite the right fit.

His childhood hadn't been easy, marred by financial difficulty, tragedy, and emotional distance. It turned him into a man who was somewhat socially awkward. He was introverted for a politician, and obviously ill-at-ease with the public. He once admitted in an interview to being *"fundamentally relatively shy."* In a letter to Pat, for example, he had mentioned *"I'm anti-social, I guess… I'd rather be by myself as a steady diet rather than with most any of the people I know…"* Glad-handing and small talk were difficult for him too.

A Meteoric Rise

Still, he rose up in politics more or less spectacularly. Richard Nixon was engaged by a group of prominent Republicans from Whittier, who were influential in encouraging him to run against five-term, incumbent liberal Democrat, Jerry Voorhis. Using fears over Voorhis' alleged sympathies for communism, he secured the win for California's 12th district, and occupied a seat in the U.S. House of Representatives in November, 1946. He moved to Washington along with his wife and young baby – Patricia was born earlier in the year, in February. The Nixons made a home for themselves there, and re-election would come easily in 1948.

As a Congressman, some of his most notable works included a stint with the Select Committee on Foreign Aid, a duty which brought him to Europe in relation to the Marshall Plan. He came into national prominence as a member of the House Un-American Activities Committee ("HUAC"), when he had a major role in the investigation of former State Department official Alger Hiss, who was accused of spying for the Soviet Union. He questioned the once-stellar diplomat, and extracted testimony that would ultimately bring Hiss to a perjury charge and several years in prison. Nixon was on the national stage, and gaining an anti-Communist reputation.

In 1950, he won decisively over Democratic Congresswoman Helen Gahagan Douglas, securing a California Senate seat. The heated campaign had Nixon again playing the anti-Communist card, accusing the other candidate of sympathy for the left. Nixon would earn his "Tricky Dick" nickname here, but that wouldn't hamper his victory, nor the rise of his political career.

His fervent anti-Communist stance captured even more national attention, and appealed among many conservatives. Soon, Republican presidential candidate, General Dwight Eisenhower was knocking on his door, too. In 1952, Richard Nixon of Yorba Linda, son of a lemon farmer and service station owner, would be the Republican candidate's running mate for vice president.

The one snag in his rise at this period were allegations of a secret slush fund set up by campaign donors angling for influence.

Nixon appeared on television to defend himself against these accusations of fiscal impropriety. He shared his financial history, and even managed to humanize himself by saying the only campaign gift he meant to personally keep was Checkers, a cocker spaniel who was beloved by the family. "The Checkers Speech" was a genius of understanding his base of political supporters, and the Republican party kept him on the ticket.

By November 1952, he and Eisenhower were walking into a victory, defeating by seven million votes, their Democratic counterparts, Illinois Governor Adlai Stevenson and running mate, Alabama Senator John Sparkman. They would also be re-elected in 1956.

The years he spent in the Vice Presidential post wasn't merely decorative for Nixon, upon whom the position acquired more visibility and consequence. He was close to the highest post in the land now, and he was able to show what he could do. He headed National Security Council meetings when President Eisenhower was unable to due to several bouts of illness during his term, and Nixon traveled extensively, fostering good will for the United States and pushing American interests during the Cold War. In 1953 for example, he and Pat visited more than 30 countries in Asia and the Middle East. He was a cool customer on the road, even in the face of the occasional anti-American hostility that his travels courted. In 1958 for example, the Nixons had a close call when their motorcade was violently mobbed in Caracas, Venezuela.

One of the most memorable anecdotes about Richard Nixon as Vice President emerged during these international trips. In 1959 he was in the Soviet Union for the American National exhibition in Moscow. He had a lively exchange with Soviet Premier Nikita Khrushchev before a display of an American kitchen, where their discussion somehow escalated into ideology. "The Kitchen Debate" once again propelled Nixon into the national spotlight. He had intelligence and guts. He was a champion for freedom and the American way of life.

The next step seemed clear: a run for the presidency. Sure enough, by 1960, he secured the Republican nomination with barely any competition. He chose Henry Cabot Lodge, former Massachusetts Senator and U.S. Ambassador to the United Nations at the time, to be his vice presidential running mate. It was on this arena – for only the greatest gladiators of American politics faced each other in the battle for the Presidency – that he would be handed a heartbreaking defeat.

Losing to Camelot

Richard Nixon seemed to have a way of looking at the world that he could never shake off. Whether by his natural temperament, disadvantaged background, hard learned experiences or a combination of all three, he grew into a distrustful man who was afraid of losing what he had worked so hard to achieve. There seemed to be a constant battle he had to win, as if he was always under some sort of threat. Even when he found success later, peace was elusive. History, glimpsed through examination of thousands of hours of White House tapes, and interviews and tales gleaned from those who knew him, would look back on Richard Nixon as an intelligent man with grit and guts, but also one plagued by his own demons.

He rose up in the world by his own merits, fueled by determination and possibly also by anger and resentment for the slights he experienced in his humble beginnings. It is said that he often identified with the less-advantaged. He once reportedly described people who had everything as *"sitting on their fat butts."* In college, the club he helped establish, the Orthogonians, were for men *"working their way through school."* It was a contrast to the school's polished society that had rejected him, the Franklins. One of the most intriguing ways of looking at Nixon's character is through this lens – that of a man from a hardscrabble background going up against 'the Beautiful People,' and winning.

Nixon made a political career out of taking down elite figures, whether he was consciously aware of it or not. Jerry Voorhis, over whom he had his first political victory for a seat at the U.S. House of Representatives, was the son of a millionaire banker. Another felled Goliath, Helen Gahagan Douglas in the Senatorial race, was a famous performer and friend of the Roosevelts. Nixon's star-making turn over sophisticated diplomat Alger Hiss also fits into the narrative.

Understanding Nixon's drive from this perspective then, indicates his loss to young, handsome, privileged and just-so-inherently-cool, Massachusetts Senator John F. Kennedy for the highest office of the land, must have hit his class sensitives hard. Indeed, the Kennedy name would haunt him for a long time.

The Presidential Elections of 1960 was a landmark one for American politics and there was no going back afterwards. The race was historic in its wide-ranging use of the technology of television. The sheer power of the medium – at the time already in 88% of American households - would be on stark display in the United States' first ever televised presidential debate between the Republican candidate, Vice President

Richard Nixon, and his Democratic foil, John F. Kennedy.

Nixon, already older and not-quite as young, dynamic or handsome, was recovering from illness to boot – pale and sweaty. He also had a tendency for growing a five o'clock shadow and did not engage the services of a gifted makeup artist. Kennedy, on the other hand, was tanned, well-rested and had a touch-up courtesy of his savvy team. As the debate raged on, Kennedy also looked at the camera while Nixon was said to look to the side as he spoke to the reporters present. The latter looked shifty to the millions of people watching at home, which did not help his "Tricky Dick" reputation. Outfit choice also proved to be damaging for the Republican nom, with his light gray suit matching the backdrop and his ashen complexion, while the Democratic bet was a force in his dark, tailored suit.

Famously, post-debate polls showed that Nixon resonated with radio listeners, while TV viewers were of the belief that Kennedy was the winner. Thanks to the new medium, the telegenic JFK –dramatically less experienced, and a Catholic too at a time when this was considered a political disadvantage – held the edge for many Americans. And it was not a passing fancy either; the images crafted from that first bout would not be dimmed by the subsequent debates, even if Nixon did start to look better.

In the end, it is estimated that 40% of the United States' population watched the series of presidential debates in 1960, which made an impact in what turned out to be a very tight election. By November, 1960, Nixon lost the presidential election by the very narrow margin of 120,000 votes.

There were accusations of voter fraud in some locales, but either way, Kennedy still had a larger number of electoral votes. Nixon did not pursue further investigation, and chose instead to accept his defeat, so as not to cause a Constitutional crisis or ruin the example that free American elections set for other nations at a time when enemies of democracy would have jumped on its flaws. He was praised for his dignified acceptance, and he retreated to southern California with his family. There, he practiced law and looked back on his political career with his bestselling memoir, *Six Crises*.

Back Into the Limelight

But it seemed as if Nixon was not a man meant for quiet living. Encouraged by various Republican influencers, a reluctant Richard ran against incumbent Democratic Governor, Edmund G. "Pat" Brown, Sr. The latter won decisively, and many – possibly including Richard Nixon himself - thought that was the door closing on his political life. He was clearly distrustful of the media at this point too, accusing them of non-objective coverage and contributing to his loss. He famously said, *"You won't have Nixon to kick around anymore because, gentlemen, this is my last press conference."*

Again, he would go into retreat, this time in New York City, where he practiced law and cultivated an image as a senior statesman.

He campaigned for Republican candidates and shared his expertise in politics and international affairs- especially on the issue of the war in Vietnam, which was bringing the United States into turmoil from without and within. The war was protracted, with no clear end in sight. There were protests and sometimes even chaos on the streets, not only about Vietnam but also about civil rights, racial issues and equality for women.

The nation it seemed, was in need of an experienced hand, a calm candidate to steer them back into order. Nixon began to position himself as that steady captain – he was stability, traditional values and law and order in a time of social disorder and uncertainty. Nixon announced his bid for president in February, 1968, and locked down the party's nomination over fellow

Republicans, the Governors Ronald Reagan, Nelson Rockefeller and George Romney. He picked as his VP, Maryland's Governor Spiro Agnew. One of the strategies he successfully employed was to tap the voting power of the South, by forging a coalition including conservatives, and making promises regarding appointments that are palatable to their base.

It only helped Nixon's cause that the Vietnam-burdened incumbent President, Lyndon B. Johnson, who came into office following the assassination of John F. Kennedy in 1963, announced he was not running for another term. Kennedy's brother, Robert, former Attorney General, Senator and key presidential contender for the Democrats, was assassinated too. The party then proved divided and uninspiring in its nomination of Vice President Hubert Humphrey, who also had to face public ire over his predecessor's Vietnam policies. By the time elections rolled around, Nixon triumphed over Humphrey and George Wallace, an independent candidate.

The man who had stepped away from the limelight made a triumphant return, as the 37th President of the United States.

Political Death

By the time Richard Nixon took office in 1969, 31,000 American lives had already been lost in the Vietnam conflict that the country has been heavily embroiled in since 1965. It was costing the nation $60-$80 million per day. The American public was weary of the increasingly unpopular war, and taking their objections to the streets. Nixon had to find a peaceful, dignified exit, and the only way he could do it was to achieve *"peace with honor"* in Vietnam in a strategy dubbed "Vietnamization."

This strategy entailed strengthening the South Vietnamese government through economic development, social reform and local elections. Most importantly, it was a gradual withdrawal of American troops, while providing training and equipment to the South Vietnamese so that they could take over the responsibility of their own defense against North Vietnam and the Viet Cong guerilla intent on uniting the country under Communist rule. According to Nixon, *"The defense of freedom is everybody's business… And it is particularly the responsibility of the people whose freedom is threatened…"*

In January 1973, the Nixon administration managed to secure a peace agreement with North Vietnam. There was a ceasefire, arrangement for the return of prisoners-of-war, and U.S. troop withdrawal. America, it seemed, had finally gotten out. South Vietnam, however, would fall into the communist hands of the North by 1975.

Nixon made strides in piercing the Iron Curtain of communism in other ways. He initiated dialogue with the Chinese and reduced trade restrictions against them. He and wife Pat even made a visit to China in 1972, for talks with Chairman Mao Zedong and Premier Zhou Enlai. Trips like these, including one to the Soviet Union later in the same year, helped to ease tensions with Communist nations and became a precursor to re-forging formal diplomatic relations. He had also helped secure agreements that limited nuclear proliferation. His administration showed gravitas and savvy in the international sphere with their efforts at forging a détente. It is also notable that his courting of China and the Soviet Union preceded agreements made regarding

Vietnam in 1973; these were a play for a better position on the negotiating table.

In the Middle East, he provided extensive military assistance to Israel during the Arab-Israel "Yom Kippur War" in 1973, and in 1974 attempted to improve relations with countries in the region through his and Secretary of State Henry Kissinger's "Shuttle Diplomacy," visiting Egypt, Israel, Jordan, Saudi Arabia and Syria.

On the domestic front, he pushed for "New Federalism," a vision of the balance of power and responsibilities between the federal government and the states that gave the latter more funding and control. This thrust, for example, allowed Nixon to appease his more conservative supporters while conforming to Court orders on school desegregation, by sharing tasks with (some say shifting the burden to) local biracial committees.

He courted conservative white votes in the presidential elections, and many of his subsequent actions in office would support that slant. But some historians posit that he was actually more of a centrist figure, a relatively 'liberal' conservative. He had backed policies that set aside a percentage of construction jobs in federally-funded projects, specifically for minorities. He helped promote business development for minorities, and also supported the extended Voting Rights Act.

He pushed agendas for women too, through more female appointees, the creation of a Presidential Task Force on Women's Rights, the pursuit of sex discrimination suits in the Department of Justice, and the inclusion of guidelines against sex discrimination on federal contracts. President Nixon also had an eye toward the environment. He established the Department of Natural Resources as well as the Environmental Protection Agency, and he advocated for the Clean Air Act. In 1971, he signed into legislation the abolishment of the military draft.

The economy at the time wasn't in great shape – the Vietnam War upped domestic inflation, there was increasing unemployment and a worsening trade deficit. Nixon had to make cuts on federal spending and the defense budget, as well as impose temporary controls on wages and prices. His administration also took the dollar off the gold standard.

Nixon would take a further hit, when his peace-seeking efforts in Vietnam are undermined by the revelation that there was secret bombing and American incursion into then-neutral Cambodia, which was accused of being a sanctuary and supply route to the North Vietnamese and the Viet Cong. But in 1972, Nixon would still trounce his Democratic challenger in his bid for re-election. The tally was a dramatic 20 million more popular votes, and Electoral College count of 520 to 17, versus the liberal senator of South Dakota, George McGovern.

The landslide victory was not surprising; polls in the campaign period had Nixon squarely, some would say even overwhelmingly, in the lead. So why then, did some in the president's re-election committee feel such a compelling need to go to extremes in its moves against the Democratic Party? Why resort to illegal activities like sabotage and espionage? Who in their right mind thought it was a great idea to break into the Democratic National Election Headquarters in Watergate? And who could have foreseen how much it would change the face of American politics forever afterwards?

The Watergate Scandal

It is interesting and really rather tragic to look back on Richard Nixon's decisive victory in the light of what happens next in his history – his downfall, which began with a seemingly insignificant break-in at the Watergate Complex in Washington, D.C.

The five-building, curving riverfront complex that comprised Watergate was designed by Italian architect Luigi Moretti and DC's landscape architect Boris Timchenko. It is a mixed-use development – the first in DC – with apartments, commercial spaces, a hotel, terraces, and the office tower that would make it one of America's most infamous addresses.

Even before its links to the first and so far only presidential resignation in U.S. history, the Watergate Complex was no stranger to controversy. In 1962, Congress was flooded with letters in a campaign initiated by Protestants and Other Americans United for Separation of Church and State ("POAU").

They protested the waivers made to Washington's building code to accommodate the plans for Watergate, citing Vatican investments in the corporation may have exerted pressure on the government. Later on, it would also run afoul of the committee working on the John F. Kennedy Center for the Performing Arts. Watergate was constructed over a span of several years, and its final component was an apartment tower slated to be built adjacent to the Kennedy Center. The building would soar more than forty feet over what was tantamount to a national shrine – a fact met with much dissatisfaction from the Kennedy Center's executive committee, as well as a prominent architecture critic who believed the Center's aesthetics deserved more dignity and space. The Watergate Complex, which was designed before the Kennedy Center, however, wouldn't be much derailed; the building in question would still be completed, albeit with a few changes, to accommodate the demands of its community.

Building codes and aesthetic choices wouldn't be the last, or the biggest of its cause for infamy. On the 17th of June 1972, a motley crew of five men were arrested on the sixth floor of the Democratic National Committee ("DNC") headquarters at the Watergate Complex at 2:30 in the morning, caught in what initially looked to be some kind of a burglary.

One of them, James W. McCord, had a background working for the Central Intelligence Agency ("CIA") and the Federal

Bureau of Investigation ("FBI"). He also worked in security for the Republican National Committee and the Committee for the Re-election of the President ("CREEP"). With him were Bernard L. Barker, a Miami-based realtor who also had links with the CIA; Virgilio R. Gonzales, a locksmith from Florida who was a refugee from Fidel Castro's Cuba; and Frank A. Sturgis and Eugenio R. Martinez, who were both associates of Barker and also had CIA and anti-Castro connections.

White House press secretary, Ronald Ziegler would call it a "*third-rate* burglary." A few days after the arrest, then-head of the Nixon reelection campaign, former Attorney General John Mitchell, would deny links to the operation, and President Nixon himself would deny involvement in a later press conference.

Less than a month later however, it was reported in the news that the bank account of "Watergate burglar" Bernard L. Barker's real estate firm had received a $25,000 cashier's check that was slated for the Nixon campaign. It was the first of many breadcrumbs that would lead determined investigators and journalists to the highest office in the land.

The check was made out to Kenneth H. Dahlberg, the Nixon campaign's Midwest finance chairman. The check was reportedly turned over months prior, to either CREEP or Nixon's re-election finance chief Maurice Stans, and Dahlberg claimed no idea on how the check wound up in Barker's account.

This bank account was also found to be the source of a large recent withdrawal by Barker, of bills some of which would later be found on the five suspects after their arrest. The money trail was indeed slowly crawling its way up to the Nixon campaign and possibly into the White House.

By October of 1972, the *Washington Posts*'s legends-in-the making, Carl Bernstein and Bob Woodward, published a story about how the FBI linked the Watergate break-in to more expansive and unprecedented efforts at political spying, sabotage and abuse of power, all connected to Nixon's reelection campaign. An undercover campaign fueled by Nixon campaign contributions was said to be geared toward the disruption of other campaigns and the discrediting of potential rival candidates. The intense activities they engaged in were allegedly included invasive investigations into candidates, their families' and even their campaign workers' personal lives; creating forged letters; sabotaging campaign schedules; employing agent provocateurs; and leaking false information to the media, among a litany of other dirty tricks. The White House would be dismissive of the details divulged by the article, with a spokesman calling them *"a collection of absurdities."*

The administration weathered the early ravages of the oncoming storm, and President Nixon still managed to secure a massive reelection victory by November. The extent of the President's involvement in the illegal activities revealed so far, was still a matter of mystery.

The story was sticking, though, thanks in no small part to the dogged investigative reporting of the two journalists Woodward and Bernstein, whose efforts would eventually be immortalized in literature and film with *All the King's Men*. Their coverage would also immortalize their unnamed source, "Deep Throat," whose identity would only be discovered decades later as W. Mark Felt, a high-ranking FBI official at the time. Bringing down a corrupt and powerful administration was still an uphill battle though, and it would take them and government investigators and politicians about two years from the time of the 1972 break-in.

The first month of 1973 would kick off the trial on the break-in. By the end of January, G. Gordon Liddy and James McCord, both former Nixon aides, would be convicted for conspiracy, burglary and wiretapping. Others, including ex-CIA operative E. Howard Hunt, would plead guilty at their own trials. Big names from Nixon's administration would be culled dramatically over the next few months following the scandal too. Attorney General Richard Kleindienst, and senior White House staffers H.R. Haldeman and John Ehrlichman resigned, and White House Counsel John Dean was fired.

In May, 1973, the Watergate scandal would enter a new phase in its winding life, including finding its way into screens across America – the Senate Watergate Committee, chaired by Senator Sam Ervin, started hearings and televised them nationally. The spotlight was also on Archibald Cox, who was appointed by Attorney General-designate Elliot Richardson as the special prosecutor tasked with investigating the Nixon reelection campaign's links to the Watergate break-in. Cox, as attorney, law professor, and former U.S. Solicitor General under Presidents JFK and LBJ, was respected in his field.

"What did the president know, and when did he know it?" was the most important question to come out of these hearings. This simple but profound and unforgettable inquiry by Senator Howard Baker, a Republican from Tennessee, would go down in history as one of the most memorable questions ever raised in American politics.

What the President Knew...

Presidents of the United States of America can have good cause to record their conversations. In 1939, President Franklin Delano Roosevelt was misquoted, and became interested in ways to preserve the accuracy of his meetings and exchanges. He made recordings from the summer of 1940 to November of that same year, but he never quite eased into the practice of recording others without their knowledge – the result was just eight hours of taped conversations. The system sat mostly unused on his desk. His successor, Harry Truman, would not find much use for such a device either, racking up just ten hours of seemingly random, garbled material. Dwight Eisenhower's White House would capture even less, at just five hours. His motivations were akin to Roosevelt's, and the administration recorded exchanges as a protection during discussions of sensitive matters or with people he couldn't quite completely trust.

When JFK took office, taping at the White House leveled up for a miscellany of potential reasons. He may have wanted the same accuracy craved by FDR. Some say he may have wanted political insurance, which would have been versus the officials who criticized the Bay of Pigs operation but did not express their objections before it fell apart. Some say that he wanted to preserve an accurate account of his administration's handling of a crisis, with an eye toward writing a memoir one day. The result was hundreds of hours of conversation, jam-packed with a lot of history, from the Cuban Missile Crisis to Civil rights issues, from the Vietnam War to the nuclear powers. His successor Lyndon Johnson continued the practice of secretly recording conversations and yielded 800 hours over his five years in office. These came in handy while Johnson was in the White House, and also when he wrote his memoirs afterwards.

When President Nixon came into office after LBJ, he didn't immediately turn toward secret recording devices. It would be only more than two years afterward that he would activate his own system, as a means of keeping an accurate record of vital decisions and discussions. Unlike the manual set-ups of presidents past however, Nixon's was voice-activated and yielded a staggering 3,700 hours of conversation.

These endless hours, which President Nixon fought to keep to himself until he was compelled by the courts to do otherwise, would link him to Watergate and help bring down his presidency.

In July of 1973, congressional testimony from Alexander Butterfield, who was former presidential appointments secretary, would reveal that Nixon had been secretly recording White House calls and conversations since 1971. Nixon would thereafter reportedly order it disabled, and refuse to turn them over to the Senate Watergate Committee, or to Cox. The investigators had cause to pursue the tapes; former White House Counsel John Dean for example, had mentioned he and the President discussed Watergate a number of times. Nixon's refusal to yield them would prompt investigators to issue subpoenas for them, which the President would appeal.

A few months later, however, came "The Saturday Night Massacre" of October 20, 1973. The fateful day saw resignations from Attorney General Richardson and Deputy AG William D. Ruckelshaus, who had refused the President's orders to fire Archibald Cox. Cox would still be ousted by Solicitor General Robert Bork in accordance with the President's order. Nixon would receive wide criticism for what he did to an investigation that was supposed to be independent. Another special prosecutor, Leon Jaworski was appointed by November 1st.

The investigations continued, and specifically, the battle for access to what would be called the "Nixon Tapes" raged on. There would be subpoenaed recordings missing 18 and ½ minutes, edited transcripts submitted in lieu of the actual tapes, and by July of 1974 – a unanimous ruling from the U.S. Supreme Court rejecting the President's claims of executive privilege and requiring him to give in to the request for tape recordings.

A few days later, articles of impeachment were passed by the House Judiciary Committee, with charges of obstruction of justice, misuse of power and contempt of Congress. It would never reach the next step, which was a full House of Representatives vote, because by early August, President Richard Nixon walked away from the office he had fought so hard to reach, and paid with everything he had to keep. His resignation speech included the lines, *"I have never been a quitter. To leave office before my term is completed is abhorrent to every instinct in my body…"*

He never admitted guilt, nor did he own up to his part in the scandal. He simply said that with limited political backing and the expectation of impeachment and removal, he would need to fight to preserve himself and then cease to become an effective leader when his country needed *"a full-time president and a full-time Congress."* He was already forging a narrative of his exit – that he would counteract his own fighting instinct and sacrifice his quest for vindication, so that his country could focus on *"the great issues of peace abroad and prosperity without inflation at home."*

But there was little else for the besieged president to do. There was a "smoking gun" in the Nixon tapes he eventually had to yield. On the 23rd of June 1972, he was recorded discussing how to frustrate the investigations into the Watergate break-in of a few days prior. The President of the United States had been part of the cover-up, and the tape to prove it was now in the hands of authorities. There seemed no indication he was part of the crime itself, however; most historians would agree that he did not have foreknowledge of the break-in.

Still, the presidential participation in a cover-up was enough for him to lose his position. And the Watergate investigation yielded so much dirt on the ugly, vicious side of American politics that many in the administration and/or members of Nixon's re-election campaign would pay for with convictions and time behind bars.

Bernard Barker, one of the "Watergate burglars," pleaded guilty to wiretapping and theft, and served 14 months behind bars. Fellow "burglars" Virgilio R. Gonzalez and Frank Sturgis served 16 months for pleading guilty to various charges against them too. Another "burglar," Eugenio Martinez, got 15 months for conspiracy, burglary and wiretapping. James McCord, the ex-CIA agent and CREEP security official who rounded up the five bungling burglars served 2 months for burglary, conspiracy and wiretapping. E. Howard Hunt, who had organized the break-in, got 33 months. Fellow organizer and former FBI man, G. Gordon Liddy, got 4.5 years.

The list goes on, toward those involved with the Committee to Re-Elect the President, the unfortunately nicknamed CREEP. Deputy Director Jeb Magruder got seven months for conspiracy to obstruct justice. Former Attorney General and CREEP Director John Mitchell got 19 months for obstruction and perjury.

Over at the White House, Special Counsel to the President, Charles Colson served seven months for obstruction of justice. Chief White House Counsel John Dean would serve four. Assistant to Nixon, John Ehrlichman got 18 months for conspiracy, obstruction of justice and perjury. The disgraced President's Chief of Staff, H.R. Haldeman got 18 months for conspiracy and obstruction of justice.

President Nixon himself, on the other hand, would be pardoned by his former VP, President Ford, as early as one month following his resignation.

Legacy

Perjury. Conspiracy. Obstruction of Justice…

The laundry list of names and the repetitive charges against them would mar Richard Nixon's legacy – and the image of the American government - forever. Suddenly, the conspiracy theorists had something concrete to fear, and distrustful quacks had some occasion to be more prophetic than paranoid.

The incidents revealed in the investigations and hearings seemed to be just the tip of the iceberg. What else lay behind the political curtain? What was going on behind the scenes where the public could not see, and the perpetrators were beyond the reach of justice? There were warrantless wiretaps!

Lists were kept of the President's enemies, and of the people listed, high-ranking officials have expressed no reservations about using the "*federal machinery*" to deal with political foes. The enemies list was so wide-ranging they even included reporters who were critical of the administration, and for one reason or another, Academy Award-winning actor, Paul Newman. There was a unit of "White House Plumbers," formed to counter leaks from within, as spurred by the Pentagon Papers leak of official Daniel Ellsberg in 1971. Among the Plumbers' upstanding activities? Breaking into the LA office of the leaker's psychiatrist to access his records. And it just added insult to injury, didn't it, that President Nixon's replacement, Vice President Gerald Ford, was actually the replacement of his Vice President Spiro

Agnew, who had been embroiled in scandals of his own and resigned in 1973?

Was no one in Washington trustworthy? After the youth and hope and vigor of the late John F. Kennedy, was this what the Office of the President was reduced to? What was left of American politics, for the American people to trust and admire?

But the erosion of the appearance and reputation of the office he had tarnished seemed to be the least of Nixon's concerns following his resignation. When he left public office, he spent his life repairing his own image by writing memoirs and books, as well as consulting with other government officials, including sharing advice with the five American Presidents that followed him. He was a prolific writer and a bestselling one. His memoir, *RN: the Memoirs of Richard Nixon*, released in 1978, was a bestseller. He would go on to write many other books over the next few years on American foreign policy and international affairs, racking up a total of ten before his death in 1994.

He achieved some success in his image rehabilitation; when the Richard Nixon Library and Birthplace was dedicated in 1990, he was there along with several Presidents and First Ladies, along with tens of thousands of supporters. In 1994, on the 25th anniversary of his first presidential inauguration, the foreign policy think tank, Nixon Center for Peace and Freedom opened in Washington. Later that year, he suffered a stroke and died at age 81 in New York City.

Even in death, however, Nixon would not be out of the limelight. First of all, his iconic, scowling sort of "Shakespearean" features are forever preserved on a considerable amount of photo and video. From the "Checkers Speech" to the "Kitchen Debate," to the legendary television moments of the 1960 presidential debate series, his televised resignation speech and the surprising revelations of the Frost interview, this is a man whose face is simply part of media and political history. His voice too, would be immortalized in thousands of hours of White House tapes, the release of which have been phased over the last few decades such that it seemed as if there was always a new facet of "Tricky Dick" to discover. Echoes of how he ran his presidential campaign can even be found now, in Donald Trump's seemingly fractured America.

Indeed, even after death, people would continue to find Nixon in the cultural space.

A Man of Many Contradictions

One of the worst afflictions of Richard Nixon was that he sometimes turned into his own worst enemy. He was a complex man, and struggled with contradictions from within and without. He was raised on the idea of peace and tolerance, and had succeeded more than most in its pursuit on the international sphere during the tense Cold War years – yet he carried grudges, composed enemies lists and pursued them relentlessly. He was a socially-awkward introvert who preferred being alone, and this only worsened with paranoia, bitterness and distrust – yet he would enter the savagery of politics and climb to its pinnacle. He made anti-Semitic remarks, but was instrumental in the security of Israel. He made a career out of anti-communism, but opened up diplomacy with China and achieved a détente with Communist countries. He was a conservative who appealed to followers of Jim Crow, but he supported affirmative action and championed the occasional liberal policy including wider health insurance coverage and environmental protection. He was secretive and private, but kept endless hours of tapes of candid conversations that would contribute to his downfall. He would also participate in a revealing interview that would expose his sense of responsibility for what had transpired in his office during the Watergate scandal.

In 1977, Nixon sat down for one of the most compelling TV events of all-time. British television personality David Frost was known for celebrity interviews, such as those he conducted with the Beatles and Muhammad Ali. The man with whom he would be dueling with was former U.S. President Richard Nixon - sharp, intelligent, an experienced politician and debater. It was Nixon's first interview following his record-setting resignation. Critics did not quite expect much substance to come out of the interview, but they would be proven very, *very* wrong.

The duelists were serious in their preparations. Nixon had a crack team poring through Watergate documents for potential questions and answers. Frost had veteran journalists on his corner, and even pored through "new" records that went unused at the trial. The ratings were huge and the stakes, massive. It was after all, in many ways, the only a cross-examination of ex-President Nixon.

Among the unforgettable, searing lines the interview would draw? *"Well, when the president does it, that means that it is not illegal…"* and Nixon wasn't even speaking of Watergate.

As for the incident that would bring about Nixon's downfall, David Frost's interview is the only venue where the former President would acknowledge his part in the Watergate cover-up. He mentioned he went *"right to the edge of the law"* in some words to staff regarding the case, and how *"a reasonable person could call that a cover up."* He would talk about how he failed to meet the responsibility of *"acting primarily in my role as the chief law enforcement officer"* at that time.

It was a breathtaking moment in television, and would later be immortalized on film with the critically-acclaimed and commercially-successful (if not entirely historically-accurate) 2008 movie, *Frost/Nixon*. Frank Langella as Nixon would go on to win awards for his performance.

The President and the times he lived in were of such a compelling nature that they would be the subject of a surprisingly varied array of movies. In 1976, when the Watergate scandal and the President's resignation was still relatively fresh, *All the President's Men* came out, based on the book by the *Washington Post*'s by-now legendary journalists, Carl Bernstein and Bob Woodward. Starring superstars Dustin Hoffman and Robert Redford, the film earned four Academy Awards. 1995's *Nixon* by Oliver Stone, depicts a biography rather than a moment in time. It starred acclaimed actor Anthony Hopkins, and depicted Nixon's paranoia, loneliness and isolation. In 1999, young stars Kirsten Dunst and Michelle Williams showed some levity with the high school-friendly, fictional *Dick*, embroiling the girls' misadventures in the key events of Watergate. "Tricky Dick" is portrayed comically here.

If these movies were a barometer of Nixon's mixed legacy, then over the years we have seen him as complex, daring, highly intelligent and willing to call the shots. But he was also conflicted. Paranoid. Lonely.

He'd been considered a malevolent, distant presence, but he was also a caricature, a rubber mask of a man, the comic depiction of the fears held by a nation. How this might be received by the late ex-President is interesting to imagine. He had, after all, long been aware of the battle for his image and legacy and how he would be viewed across the lens of time.

As early as 1971, he expressed concerns about the inflated myths surrounding John F. Kennedy, and his own frustrations with how he was coming across with the public. He wanted to be known for "*Courage, boldness, guts…*" Nixon, clearly, is a polarizing figure. But if there is anything people can agree on, it is probably that these are virtues no one can begrudge the disgraced ex-President.

He was born into tough circumstances in a time of war. It was already an achievement to survive and make his own way in the world, but he pursued and excelled in education. He married the girl he always said he would. He pressed himself into more and more active, dangerous service in the War. He overcame his humble origins and doggedly made his way into Washington, taking down elites as he went. He became the President of the most powerful country in the world – elected twice, the second by a stunning margin. He left office in disgrace, but dodged the harsh penalties foisted on others. He wrote ten books, and somehow still ended up with four Presidents in his funeral, and he is buried next to his wife in a library under his name.

Courage. Boldness. Guts.

Not always geared toward what was right, sometimes skirting 'right to the edge of the law' so to speak, and he was sometimes inconsistent with where he applied his considerable energies, but he at the very least, embodied that.

Lingering Impact in American Politics

It's been over 100 years since Nixon's birth in 1913. It's been over 40 years since he resigned, and over 20 years since he died. But in a fractured America that is currently run by one polarizing Mr. Donald Trump, there are still traces of "Tricky Dick" to be found, and lessons to be learned.

Richard Nixon was a genius at playing demographics in the elections and had a great sense of how to transform fears and anxieties into support and votes – which may sounds familiar in the era of Trump's divisive, anti-Muslim, anti-immigrant politics. Furthermore, the "Southern Strategy" used in his bid for presidency, would be part of the Republican playbook for years to come. Echoes of these could also be spotted in Donald Trump's recent victory.

Aside from elections, Nixon and Watergate also had an impact on how Americans perceived their government. The scandal pulled the rug out from under America and exposed the dirty underbelly of political life. Though the erosion of public trust and our resulting cynicism of our politicians may be considered tragic, we are also less naïve, and more open to questioning authority and in some ways, that is healthy too. We have learned that democracy is not a perfect system, and that being a part of it requires discernment. This is more important than ever, as we come under constant assault from "fake news," misinformation, and other dirty tricks of politics.

The Watergate scandal, however, showed the power and importance of a free, independent press. President Nixon had been hostile to and distrusting of the media, and sometimes rather openly (which may again, sound familiar to those following the rollercoaster of Donald Trump's presidency). But Woodward and Bernstein, and other critics of the administration, could be credited with keeping the public informed and invested in a story, consequently exerting pressure on our elected officials to perform better. These are roles that are still demanded of our practitioners in the media, as well as of the public in general. We have a responsibility in how our country is run.

America's Watergate episode was an eye-opening one to many who had been alive and aware to see it unfurl. We are now at a time and age where it seems distant, but its central themes are very much still relevant. That a man of Richard Nixon's relentless drive and intelligence should have been embroiled in it is a tragedy, but even tragedies hold lessons. Hopefully, the generations to follow will not squander away all that it has to teach us.

Made in the USA
San Bernardino, CA
03 November 2019